Introduction:

Welcome to "What is AI," a comprehensive exploration of the fascinating field of Artificial Intelligence (AI). In this book, we embark on a journey to demystify AI, unravel its inner workings, and understand its profound impact on our world.

AI has become an integral part of our daily lives, from voice assistants in our smartphones to personalized recommendations on streaming platforms. But what exactly is AI? How does it work? What it can do and what are its limitations? These are questions we aim to answer in this book, catering to readers of all backgrounds, from beginners to those with a basic understanding of AI.

In this rapidly advancing technological landscape, AI has emerged as a game-changer, revolutionizing industries, shaping economies, and transforming the way we live, work, and interact. It holds immense potential to tackle complex problems, enhance decision-making, and augment human capabilities. However, it also poses ethical and societal challenges that demand careful consideration.

Our goal is to provide a comprehensive overview of AI, starting with its foundations and core principles. We will delve into the fundamental concepts, including automation, data, algorithms, machine learning, neural networks, and the importance of training and testing AI systems.

From there, we will explore the real-world applications of AI across various sectors, including healthcare, finance, transportation, manufacturing, education, entertainment, and environmental sustainability. These examples will demonstrate the diverse ways in which AI is transforming industries, improving efficiency, and creating innovative solutions.

In addition, we will dive into the future of AI, discussing emerging trends, potential challenges, and the implications for society. We will explore the advancements in AI research, the impact of automation on the job market, the potential for human augmentation, and the importance of ethical considerations, data privacy, and lifelong learning in an AI-driven world.

Throughout this book, we strive to make the topic of AI accessible and understandable to readers of all levels of expertise. We aim to demystify complex concepts, provide practical examples, and shed light on both the promises and potential pitfalls of AI.

Whether you are a student, a professional, or simply curious about AI, this book will serve as a guide to navigate the ever-evolving world of Artificial Intelligence. We invite you to join us on this captivating journey, where we unravel the mysteries of AI and explore its transformative potential.

So, let us embark on this exploration of "What is AI" and unlock the secrets of this powerful technology that is shaping our present and shaping the future.

About Author:

My name is Ajinkya Khamitkar, and I am the author of the book "What is AI." With an MBA in Information Technology and a decade of experience in the IT field, I bring a wealth of knowledge and expertise to the subject of Artificial Intelligence (AI). My passion for AI runs deep, and I am dedicated to sharing my insights with readers who are curious about this rapidly evolving field.

Throughout my educational and professional journey, I have been captivated by the potential of AI to transform industries and drive innovation. My background in Information Technology has equipped me with a solid foundation to understand the technical intricacies of AI and its practical applications.

Over the course of my career, I have had the privilege of working on numerous AI projects, witnessing firsthand how this powerful technology can automate processes, analyze data, and generate valuable insights. This hands-on experience has deepened my understanding of AI's capabilities and limitations.

In writing "What is AI," I have aimed to create a book that is accessible to readers of all backgrounds, from beginners to professionals. I believe in simplifying complex concepts and explaining them in a clear and concise manner. My goal is to provide readers with a comprehensive overview of AI, covering its foundations, principles, and real-world applications.

My keen interest in AI goes beyond its technical aspects. I am also deeply interested in the ethical implications and societal impact of AI. I believe in fostering a responsible and inclusive approach to AI development and deployment, and I address these important considerations in my book.

Beyond writing, I actively engage in ongoing learning and stay abreast of the latest advancements and trends in AI. This ensures that my knowledge remains relevant and up-to-date, allowing me to provide readers with accurate and timely information.

I am thrilled to share my passion for AI through "What is AI," and I hope that readers will find this book enlightening, engaging, and informative. Whether you are a student, professional, or simply curious about AI, I invite you to embark on this journey with me and discover the endless possibilities that AI offers.

This book is dedicated to...

My Father, My Mother, My sister and My Wife.

-Ajinkya Khamitkar

Table of content:

Chapter 8: AI and Social Impact

Social and Economic Implications of AI

Addressing AI-Induced Inequalities

AI for Social Justice and Equality

Ethical AI Applications in Education

AI and Accessibility for Persons with Disabilities

AI in Humanitarian and Development Efforts

Chapter 9: AI and the Human Mind

Understanding AI and Human Cognition

Cognitive Computing and AI

AI in Brain-Computer Interfaces

AI and Mental Health

Ethical Considerations in AI-Enhanced Human Mind Interfaces

Challenges and Opportunities for AI and the Human Mind

Chapter 10: AI in Space Exploration and Research

AI in Space Exploration Missions

Autonomous Rovers and Robots in Space

AI-Enabled Data Analysis and Interpretation

AI for Astronomical Research and Discoveries

Ethical Considerations in AI-Assisted Space Exploration

The Future of AI in Advancing Space Research

Chapter 1: Introduction to Artificial Intelligence

Welcome to the amazing world of Artificial Intelligence (AI)! In this chapter, we will explore the fundamental concepts and key aspects of AI, providing a simple and beginner-friendly introduction to this fascinating field.

1: What is Artificial Intelligence?

Artificial Intelligence, often abbreviated as AI, is the part of computer science that focuses on creating intelligent systems and machines which are capable of performing tasks that typically require the human brain and intelligence. These tasks can range from simple calculations to complex problem-solving and decision-making.

2: The Origins of AI

The concept of AI emerged in the 1950s when researchers began to explore the possibility of creating machines that could mimic human intelligence. Over the years, advancements in computer technology and the development of sophisticated algorithms have propelled the field forward.

3: Understanding Intelligence

To understand AI better, let's first delve into the concept of intelligence itself. Intelligence refers to the ability to acquire knowledge, understand, reason, and apply that knowledge to solve problems. Human intelligence encompasses various cognitive abilities, such as perception, learning, language processing, and decision-making.

4: Types of AI

AI can be classified into two primary categories: Narrow AI and General AI. Narrow AI, also known as Weak AI, is designed to perform specific tasks with high proficiency, such as voice recognition, image classification, or playing chess. On the other hand, General AI aims to possess the same level of intelligence and versatility as human beings, capable of understanding and performing any intellectual task.

5: Machine Learning

Machine Learning is a critical subfield of AI that involves the development of algorithms and models that let computers learn from it and make predictions or decisions which is based on available data. It empowers machines to improve their performance over time without being explicitly programmed.

6: Deep Learning

Deep Learning is a subset of Machine Learning that focuses on training artificial neural networks with multiple layers to process complex data and extract meaningful patterns. Inspired by the human brain, deep learning has revolutionized AI, enabling breakthroughs in areas like image recognition, natural language processing, and autonomous driving.

7: Real-World Applications

AI has made significant strides in various domains, enhancing our lives and transforming industries. Some notable applications include:

Virtual Assistants: Intelligent personal assistants like Siri, Alexa, and Google Assistant that can understand and respond to human voice commands.

Recommendation Systems: Algorithms that suggest products, movies, or music based on individual preferences and behavior patterns.

Healthcare: AI is being employed to improve disease diagnosis, drug discovery, and personalized medicine.

Autonomous Vehicles: Self-driving cars that use AI algorithms to perceive the environment and make real-time driving decisions.

Natural Language Processing: AI systems that can understand, process, and generate human language, enabling chatbots and translation services.

Conclusion:

Artificial Intelligence is a vast and rapidly evolving field that has the potential to revolutionize the way we live, work, and interact with technology. In this chapter, we have laid the foundation by exploring the basics of AI, its origins, types, and real-world applications. In the subsequent chapters, we will dive deeper into the core concepts and explore how AI is shaping various industries and our future.

Remember, this is just the beginning of your journey into the intriguing world of AI. Stay curious, ask questions, and keep exploring the endless possibilities that AI offers.

In the next chapter, we will explore the evolution of AI and its impact on society.

Chapter 2: The Evolution of AI and Its Impact on Society

Welcome back to our exploration of Artificial Intelligence (AI). In this chapter, we will delve into the evolution of AI, tracing its historical milestones and examining its profound impact on society. Prepare to discover the remarkable journey that has brought us to the AI-powered world we live in today.

1: Early Beginnings

The roots of AI can be traced back to the 1950s when researchers began envisioning machines that could mimic human intelligence. It was during this time that the term "Artificial Intelligence" was coined, sparking excitement and curiosity about the possibilities that lay ahead.

2: The AI Winter

Despite the initial enthusiasm, the progress of AI faced significant challenges and setbacks in the 1970s and 1980s. These challenging periods, often referred to as the "AI Winter," were characterized by limited funding, unfulfilled expectations, and a lack of practical applications. However, these difficult times also led to valuable lessons and a reevaluation of AI's goals and approaches.

3: The Rise of Machine Learning

In the 1990s and early 2000s, AI experienced a resurgence, largely due to advancements in Machine Learning. Researchers shifted their focus from rule-based systems to developing algorithms that could learn from data. This shift opened up new possibilities and paved the way for significant breakthroughs in AI research.

4: Big Data and AI

The explosion of digital data in recent years has played a pivotal role in advancing AI capabilities. With the advent of the internet and the proliferation of connected devices, vast amounts of data became available for analysis. AI algorithms, particularly those based on Machine Learning, thrived on this wealth of information, fueling advancements in areas like image recognition, natural language processing, and predictive analytics.

5: AI in Everyday Life

AI has infiltrated our daily lives, often without us even realizing it. From personalized recommendations on streaming platforms to voice assistants on our smartphones, AI has become an integral part of our digital experiences. Additionally, AI has found its way into industries such as healthcare, finance, transportation, and manufacturing, revolutionizing processes, improving efficiency, and enhancing decision-making.

6: Ethical Considerations

As AI continues to evolve and expand its reach, ethical considerations have come to the forefront. Questions surrounding privacy, bias, transparency, and job displacement have prompted discussions and debates. It is essential to navigate these ethical challenges and ensure that AI is developed and deployed responsibly, with the best interests of humanity in mind.

7: The Future of AI

The future of AI holds immense potential. Advancements in areas such as Deep Learning, Reinforcement Learning, and Explainable AI are driving the field forward. The possibilities of AI are vast, ranging from autonomous vehicles and robotics to personalized healthcare and climate change mitigation. It is an exciting time to witness the evolution of AI and be a part of shaping its future.

Conclusion:

In this chapter, we explored the evolution of AI, from its early beginnings to its current pervasive presence in society. We witnessed the challenges faced by AI and the subsequent breakthroughs that propelled the field forward. AI has transformed the way we live, work, and interact with technology, and its impact will only continue to grow.

As we move forward, it is crucial to understand AI's potential and the ethical considerations that come with it. The future of AI holds immense promise, and we must harness its power responsibly, ensuring that it aligns with our values and benefits humanity as a whole.

In the next chapter, we will dive deeper into the core principles of AI and explore the key concepts that drive its functionality. Stay curious and get ready to unlock the inner workings of this remarkable technology.

Chapter 3: Core Principles of AI

Welcome to the third chapter of our book, where we will explore the core principles that underpin Artificial Intelligence (AI). Understanding these principles is essential for grasping the inner workings of AI systems and how they make decisions. So, let's dive in!

1: Automation and Task Performance

At its core, AI aims to automate tasks that typically require human intelligence. Whether it's recognizing images, understanding natural language, or driving a car, AI systems are designed to perform these tasks with speed, accuracy, and efficiency. By automating these tasks, AI frees up human resources and enables us to tackle more complex challenges.

2: Data and Algorithms

Data is the lifeblood of AI. AI systems learn and make predictions based on vast amounts of data. These data sets are fed into algorithms, which are sets of instructions that guide the AI's learning and decision-making processes. The quality and diversity of the data, combined with the sophistication of the algorithms, play a crucial role in the effectiveness of AI systems.

3: Machine Learning Algorithms

Machine Learning is a key component of AI, enabling systems to learn from data and improve their performance over time. There are three important types of Machine Learning algorithms:

i). Supervised Learning: In this approach, the AI system is trained on labeled examples, where the desired output is provided for each input. Through this training, the AI system learns to generalize and make predictions on new, unseen data.

ii). Unsupervised Learning: Unlike supervised learning, unsupervised learning involves training an AI system on unlabeled data. The system analyzes patterns, structures, and relationships within the data to uncover hidden insights and make sense of the information.

iii). Reinforcement Learning: This type of learning involves an AI agent interacting with an environment. The agent receives feedback in the form of some rewards or punishments based on its actions. Through trial and error, the agent learns to maximize rewards and make optimal decisions.

4: Neural Networks

Neural networks are a fundamental component of AI systems, inspired by the structure and functioning of the human brain. These networks consist of interconnected nodes called neurons, organized in layers. Neural networks excel in tasks such as image and speech recognition, natural language processing, and decision-making.

5: Training and Testing To develop an effective AI system, training and testing are crucial steps. During the training phase, the AI system learns from labeled or unlabeled data, adjusting its parameters and optimizing its performance. The testing phase evaluates the system's accuracy, generalization, and robustness on new, unseen data. This iterative process allows AI systems to continuously improve their performance.

6: Explain ability and Interpretability

The ability to explain and interpret AI decisions is becoming increasingly important. As AI systems become more complex, understanding how they arrive at their conclusions is vital, especially in critical domains like healthcare and finance. Researchers are actively working on developing methods to make AI systems more transparent, interpretable, and accountable.

7: Human-AI Collaboration

AI is not meant to replace humans; instead, it has the potential to augment our abilities and enable collaboration. Human-AI collaboration involves leveraging the strengths of both humans and AI systems to solve complex problems, make informed decisions, and achieve better outcomes.

Conclusion:

In this chapter, we explored the core principles of AI, including automation, data, algorithms, machine learning, neural networks, training, testing, explain ability, and human-AI collaboration. Understanding these principles provides a foundation for comprehending how AI systems work and the possibilities they offer.

AI is a powerful tool that has the potential to transform various industries and enhance our lives in numerous ways. As we move forward, it is crucial to embrace AI's capabilities while also considering

Chapter 4: Real-World Applications of AI

Welcome to the fourth chapter of our book on Artificial Intelligence (AI). In this chapter, we will explore the diverse and exciting real-world applications of AI across various industries and sectors. From healthcare to finance, transportation to entertainment, AI is transforming the way we live and work. Let's dive in and discover the incredible possibilities!

1: Healthcare

AI has the potential to revolutionize healthcare by improving diagnostics, personalized treatment plans, and patient care. AI-powered systems can analyze medical images, such as X-rays and MRIs, aiding in early detection of diseases. AI algorithms can also analyze patient data to identify patterns and provide personalized treatment recommendations.

2: Finance

In the financial sector, AI is used for fraud detection, risk assessment, and algorithmic trading. Machine Learning algorithms analyze vast amounts of financial data to identify suspicious transactions and patterns indicative of fraud. AI-powered robo-advisors offer personalized financial advice based on an individual's financial goals and risk tolerance.

3: Transportation

AI is reshaping transportation with advancements in autonomous vehicles and smart traffic management systems. Self-driving cars use AI algorithms to perceive their environment, make real-time decisions, and navigate safely. Intelligent traffic systems leverage AI to optimize traffic flow, reduce congestion, and improve transportation efficiency.

4: Manufacturing and Robotics

AI is revolutionizing manufacturing processes with the introduction of intelligent robots and automation. Robots equipped with AI capabilities can perform complex tasks with precision and speed, enhancing efficiency and productivity. AI-powered systems can analyze sensor data to detect anomalies, predict maintenance needs, and optimize production.

5: Natural Language Processing

Natural Language Processing (NLP) let machines to understand and interact with human language. Virtual assistants, such as Siri and Alexa, leverage NLP to comprehend voice commands and provide responses. Chatbots use NLP algorithms to engage in human-like conversations, assisting with customer support and information retrieval.

6: Education

AI is making strides in the field of education, offering personalized learning experiences and intelligent tutoring systems. Adaptive learning platforms use AI algorithms to analyze students' performance data and tailor educational content to their individual needs and learning styles. AI-powered chatbots provide instant support and guidance to students.

7: Entertainment and Gaming

AI has transformed the entertainment industry by enhancing user experiences and creating immersive content. Streaming services use AI algorithms to recommend personalized movies, TV shows, and music based on user preferences. AI is also employed in game development to create intelligent and dynamic virtual characters and opponents.

8: Environmental Sustainability

AI is playing a vital role in addressing environmental challenges. It is used for climate modeling, predicting natural disasters, optimizing energy consumption, and managing waste. AI-powered systems can analyze environmental data to identify patterns and trends, enabling better resource management and conservation efforts.

Conclusion:

In this chapter, we explored the diverse applications of AI in various industries and sectors. From healthcare to finance, transportation to entertainment, AI is driving innovation and transforming the way we live and work. Its potential is vast, and its impact is only expected to grow in the coming years.

As AI continues to evolve, it is crucial to harness its capabilities responsibly, ensuring transparency, fairness, and ethical considerations. The real-world applications of AI have the power to improve efficiency, enhance decision-making, and create new possibilities across numerous domains.

In the next chapter, we will explore the future of AI, examining emerging trends and potential challenges. Join us as we embark on this journey into the exciting frontier of Artificial Intelligence.

Chapter 5: The Future of AI

Welcome to the final chapter of our book on Artificial Intelligence (AI). In this chapter, we will explore the future of AI, examining emerging trends, potential challenges, and the profound impact AI is likely to have on our lives. Get ready to glimpse into the exciting possibilities that lie ahead!

1: Advancements in AI Research

AI research and development continue to push boundaries and uncover new possibilities. Emerging areas such as Explainable AI, Quantum AI, and Edge Computing are poised to revolutionize the field. Researchers are striving to make AI systems more transparent, interpretable, and accountable, addressing ethical concerns and building trust.

2: AI and Automation

The integration of AI into various industries will lead to increased automation, transforming the nature of work. While some jobs may be replaced by AI, new roles will emerge, requiring skills in managing AI systems, interpreting insights, and collaborating with intelligent machines. It is crucial to foster a workforce that is adaptable and equipped for the evolving AI landscape.

3: AI and Human Augmentation

AI has the potential to augment human capabilities, enabling us to achieve new heights. From healthcare to education, AI-powered tools can enhance decision-making, personalize learning experiences, and provide assistance in various domains. The collaboration between humans and AI can lead to innovative solutions and amplify our collective potential.

4: Ethical Considerations and Regulation

As AI becomes more prevalent, addressing ethical considerations and establishing robust regulations become imperative. Transparency, fairness, privacy, and accountability are critical aspects that need to be carefully navigated. Collaboration between policymakers, technologists, and ethicists is crucial to ensure that AI is developed and deployed in a responsible and beneficial manner.

5: AI for Social Good

AI has the potential to address societal challenges and contribute to social good. From healthcare accessibility to poverty alleviation, AI-powered solutions can make a positive impact on society. It is essential to prioritize the development and deployment of AI systems that are inclusive, equitable, and focused on benefiting humanity as a whole.

6: AI and Data Privacy

With the increasing reliance on data for AI systems, protecting individual privacy becomes paramount. Striking a balance between utilizing data for AI advancements and respecting user privacy is a challenge that needs to be addressed. Innovations in privacy-preserving techniques and regulations can help ensure that AI respects individual rights and maintains trust.

7: Lifelong Learning and AI

As AI advances, the importance of lifelong learning becomes evident. Continuous learning and upskilling will empower individuals to adapt to the changing job market and harness the potential of AI. Educational institutions and governments need to prioritize accessible and relevant education programs that enable individuals with the necessary skills to thrive in an AI-driven world.

Conclusion:

In this final chapter, we explored the future of AI, highlighting emerging trends, challenges, and the transformative impact AI is likely to have on society. The future of AI holds immense promise, with advancements in research, automation, human augmentation, and social good. However, it is crucial to navigate ethical considerations, and privacy concerns, and foster a collaborative approach to ensure a responsible and beneficial AI future.

As we embark on this AI journey, it is important to embrace the potential of AI while also acknowledging the human-centric approach. AI is a tool that can amplify human abilities, solve complex problems, and create a better future for all.

Remember, AI is an evolving field, and the future is filled with opportunities and challenges. Stay curious, remain informed, and actively engage in shaping the future of AI to create a world that is both technologically advanced and human-centric.

Chapter 6: The Ethical Implications of AI

This chapter delves into the role of Artificial Intelligence (AI) in governance and public policy. It explores how AI is transforming the way governments operate, deliver public services, and make policy decisions. The chapter examines the ethical and legal implications of AI in the public sector, emphasizing the need for transparency, accountability, and bias mitigation. It also discusses the importance of regulating AI to ensure responsible and ethical use in governance. Overall, this chapter provides insights into the impact of AI on governance and highlights the challenges and considerations that arise in leveraging AI technologies for public benefit.

The Role of AI in Governance:

This section delves into the role of AI in governance, highlighting how AI technologies can automate administrative processes, improve policy formulation, and enhance citizen engagement. It emphasizes the potential of AI to optimize government operations and decision-making processes.

AI in Public Service Delivery:

The chapter explores how AI is revolutionizing public service delivery. It discusses the use of AI-powered technologies, such as chatbots and virtual assistants, to provide personalized and efficient services to citizens. It also examines the application of AI in sectors like healthcare, transportation, and education, enhancing the overall quality of public services.

AI for Policy Analysis and Decision-Making:

This part focuses on how AI can be utilized for policy analysis and decision-making. It highlights the ability of AI algorithms to analyze vast amounts of data, generate insights, and inform policy formulation. It emphasizes the complementary role of AI in supporting human decision-making, ensuring that policy decisions consider both AI-generated insights and human judgment.

Ethical & Legal Implications:

The chapter explores the ethical and legal implications of AI in the public sector. It discusses concerns related to fairness, accountability, and privacy, emphasizing the need for ethical guidelines and legal frameworks to govern the use of AI. It addresses issues such as algorithmic bias, the responsible use of data, and the protection of citizens' rights in the context of AI-driven governance.

Transparency, Accountability, and Bias Mitigation:

This section highlights the importance of transparency, accountability, and bias mitigation in AI-driven governance. It discusses the need for AI systems to provide explanations for their decisions and be auditable. It emphasizes the identification and mitigation of bias in AI systems to ensure fairness and avoid discriminatory outcomes.

Regulating AI in the Public Sector:

The chapter examines the challenges and approaches to regulating AI in the public sector. It discusses the establishment of regulatory frameworks to govern the development, deployment, and use of AI technologies. It emphasizes the collaboration between government agencies, industry stakeholders, and experts in creating guidelines and standards for responsible AI governance.

Conclusion:

This chapter demonstrates the transformative potential of AI in governance and public policy. By leveraging AI technologies, governments can improve public service delivery, enhance decision-making processes, and optimize resource allocation. However, it also emphasizes the need to address ethical and legal considerations and establish regulatory frameworks to ensure responsible and ethical use of AI in the public sector. By doing so, governments can harness the benefits of AI while upholding principles of fairness, transparency, and accountability, ultimately creating more effective and citizen-centric governance.

Chapter 7: AI and Cybersecurity

This chapter delves into the relationship between Artificial Intelligence (AI) and cybersecurity. It explores how AI technologies are transforming the field of cybersecurity, both in terms of threat detection and prevention, as well as defense strategies. The chapter highlights the importance of enhancing data security and privacy in the digital age and examines the ethical considerations associated with AI-driven cybersecurity. Furthermore, it discusses the future of AI in cybersecurity and explores emerging trends and advancements in the field.

The Intersection of AI and Cybersecurity:

This section explores the intersection of AI and cybersecurity. It discusses how AI technologies are being integrated into cybersecurity practices to bolster defense mechanisms, detect threats, and respond to cyber-attacks. It highlights the growing significance of AI in the context of cybersecurity and its potential to revolutionize the field.

AI for Threat Detection & Prevention:

The chapter focuses on how AI is utilized for threat detection and prevention. It explains how AI algorithms can analyze vast amounts of data, identify patterns, and detect anomalies that signify potential cyber threats. The use of AI in areas such as network monitoring, intrusion detection, and malware analysis is discussed, highlighting its role in proactively mitigating cybersecurity risks.

Enhancing Data Security and Privacy:

Data security and privacy are critical considerations in the digital landscape. This part explores how AI can enhance data security through techniques such as encryption, access control, and anomaly detection. It highlights the use of AI-powered tools and technologies to safeguard sensitive data, ensuring its confidentiality and integrity.

AI-Powered Cyberattacks and Defense Strategies:

While AI can be employed for defensive purposes, it can also be utilized in cyberattacks. This section examines the potential of AI-powered cyberattacks, such as automated phishing campaigns, advanced social engineering, and AI-generated deepfake attacks. It emphasizes the need to develop robust defense strategies and countermeasures to mitigate the risks associated with AI-driven cyber threats.

Ethical Considerations in AI-Driven Cybersecurity:

The adoption of AI in cybersecurity raises ethical considerations that must be addressed. This part explores the ethical implications of AI-driven cybersecurity, including algorithmic bias, privacy infringements, and the responsible use of AI in offensive cybersecurity operations. It underscores the importance of ethical AI practices, transparency, and accountability in ensuring ethical cybersecurity practices.

The Future of AI in Cybersecurity:

The chapter concludes by discussing the future of AI in cybersecurity. It examines emerging trends and advancements in AI technologies, such as machine learning, natural language processing, and behavioral analytics, that can strengthen cybersecurity defenses. It emphasizes the need for ongoing research, collaboration, and education to stay ahead in the evolving landscape of AI-driven cyber threats.

Conclusion:

This chapter explores the vital role that AI plays in cybersecurity, from threat detection and prevention to data security and privacy enhancement. It also addresses the ethical considerations associated with AI-driven cybersecurity and provides insights into the future of AI in this field. By understanding the intersection of AI and cybersecurity, organizations can harness the power of AI to strengthen their defenses and protect against evolving cyber threats.

Chapter 8: AI and Social Impact

This chapter of "What is AI" explores the social impact of Artificial Intelligence (AI) and its implications for society. It examines how AI technologies influence various aspects of social life, including social and economic dynamics, inequalities, social justice, education, accessibility, and humanitarian efforts. The chapter emphasizes the ethical considerations surrounding AI applications and highlights the potential of AI to contribute positively to social development and equality.

Social and Economic Implications of AI:

This section delves into the social and economic implications of AI. It discusses how AI adoption affects employment, job displacement, and the changing nature of work. It also explores the potential economic benefits and challenges associated with AI implementation, such as productivity improvements and income inequality.

Addressing AI-Induced Inequalities:

The chapter highlights the importance of addressing AI-induced inequalities. It explores how biases and limitations in AI systems can perpetuate existing societal inequalities and emphasizes the need for fairness and equity in AI algorithms and applications. Strategies for mitigating biases and promoting inclusive AI systems are discussed.

AI for Social Justice and Equality:

This part examines the potential of AI to promote social justice and equality. It explores how AI can be leveraged to address social challenges, such as poverty, discrimination, and access to basic services. It showcases examples of AI initiatives that aim to tackle societal issues and promote a more equitable society.

Ethical AI Applications in Education:

The chapter explores the ethical applications of AI in the field of education. It discusses how AI can enhance learning experiences, personalize education, and provide intelligent tutoring. It also addresses concerns regarding privacy, data security, and ethical considerations in utilizing AI in educational settings.

AI and Accessibility for Persons with Disabilities:

This section focuses on the impact of AI on accessibility for persons with disabilities. It discusses how AI technologies can improve accessibility by providing assistive technologies, enabling communication, and enhancing mobility for individuals with disabilities. It highlights the potential of AI to create inclusive environments and empower people with disabilities.

AI in Humanitarian and Development Efforts:

The chapter concludes by examining the role of AI in humanitarian and development efforts. It explores how AI can be utilized to address global challenges, such as disaster response, healthcare access, and resource allocation in developing regions. It showcases examples of AI applications in humanitarian contexts and emphasizes the potential for AI to make a positive social impact.

Conclusion:

This chapter provides an in-depth analysis of the social impact of AI, addressing topics such as economic implications, inequalities, social justice, education, accessibility, and humanitarian efforts. By understanding the potential of AI to influence society, readers gain insights into the ethical considerations and opportunities for leveraging AI to create a more inclusive, just, and equitable world.

Chapter 9: AI and the Human Mind

This chapter of "What is AI" explores the intersection between Artificial Intelligence (AI) and the human mind. It examines how AI technologies are advancing our understanding of human cognition, facilitating cognitive computing, and influencing brain-computer interfaces. The chapter also discusses the application of AI in mental health and highlights the ethical considerations surrounding AI-enhanced human mind interfaces. Lastly, it explores the challenges and opportunities presented by the integration of AI and the human mind.

Understanding AI and Human Cognition:

This section provides an overview of AI and its relationship with human cognition. It discusses how AI algorithms and models are designed to simulate and understand human cognitive processes, such as perception, learning, and problem-solving. It explores the parallels between AI and human intelligence, shedding light on the potential for AI to enhance our understanding of the human mind.

Cognitive Computing and AI:

The chapter explores the field of cognitive computing and its connection to AI. It explains how cognitive computing systems leverage AI technologies to process vast amounts of data, interpret complex information, and simulate human-like cognitive abilities. It showcases real-world applications of cognitive computing and its potential to augment human intelligence.

AI in Brain-Computer Interfaces:

This part delves into the integration of AI in brain-computer interfaces (BCIs). It discusses how AI algorithms can interpret neural signals and facilitate communication between the human brain and external devices. It explores the advancements in AI-powered BCIs and their potential to enhance mobility, restore sensory functions, and assist individuals with disabilities.

AI and Mental Health:

The chapter examines the role of AI in the field of mental health. It discusses how AI technologies, such as natural language processing and machine learning, can analyze behavioral patterns and provide insights into mental health conditions. It explores the use of AI-powered tools for early detection, diagnosis, and personalized treatment in mental healthcare.

Ethical Considerations in AI-Enhanced Human Mind Interfaces:

The integration of AI with the human mind raises ethical considerations. This section explores the ethical implications of AI-enhanced human mind interfaces, such as privacy, consent, and the potential for manipulation or exploitation. It emphasizes the need for ethical guidelines and responsible use of AI technologies in this domain.

Challenges and Opportunities for AI and the Human Mind:

The chapter concludes by discussing the challenges and opportunities presented by the integration of AI and the human mind. It examines the potential benefits of AI in enhancing cognitive abilities, improving mental healthcare, and fostering human-AI collaboration. It also addresses challenges, including the potential for bias and the need for ongoing research and regulation to ensure safe and ethical use of AI in the context of the human mind.

Conclusion:

This chapter provides a comprehensive exploration of the relationship between AI and the human mind. By examining cognitive computing, brain-computer interfaces, mental health applications, ethical considerations, and the challenges and opportunities that arise, readers gain insights into the potential of AI to augment human cognition and contribute to advancements in mental health and well-being.

Chapter 10: AI in Space Exploration and Research

This chapter of "What is AI" delves into the fascinating realm of AI in space exploration and research. It explores how Artificial Intelligence (AI) is transforming space missions by enabling autonomous rovers and robots, facilitating data analysis and interpretation, and advancing astronomical research. The chapter also addresses the ethical considerations associated with AI-assisted space exploration and provides insights into the future of AI in pushing the boundaries of space research.

AI in Space Exploration Missions:

This section highlights the role of AI in space exploration missions. It discusses how AI technologies are integrated into spacecraft systems, enabling autonomous decision-making, navigation, and hazard avoidance. It explores the benefits of AI in optimizing mission efficiency and adaptability, as well as reducing human intervention in space exploration endeavors.

Autonomous Rovers and Robots in Space:

The chapter focuses on the application of AI in autonomous rovers and robots for space exploration. It showcases how AI algorithms enable these robotic systems to navigate challenging terrains, collect data, and make intelligent decisions in real-time. It highlights the advancements in AI-powered robotic exploration and their contributions to our understanding of celestial bodies.

AI-Enabled Data Analysis and Interpretation:

This part explores how AI enhances data analysis and interpretation in space research. It discusses how AI algorithms and machine learning techniques can analyze vast amounts of space data, identify patterns, and extract valuable insights. It showcases the use of AI in understanding cosmic phenomena, identifying celestial objects, and uncovering hidden relationships within astronomical datasets.

AI for Astronomical Research and Discoveries:

The chapter explores the impact of AI in advancing astronomical research and discoveries. It highlights how AI algorithms can assist in identifying exoplanets, analyzing stellar spectra, and detecting celestial events. It showcases how AI is revolutionizing our ability to explore the cosmos and discover new celestial phenomena.

Ethical Considerations in AI-Assisted Space Exploration:

The integration of AI in space exploration raises ethical considerations. This section addresses the ethical implications associated with AI-assisted space exploration, including issues related to privacy, data sharing, and the potential impact on indigenous space ecosystems. It emphasizes the importance of responsible and ethical practices in utilizing AI technologies in space research.

The Future of AI in Advancing Space Research:

The chapter concludes by discussing the future of AI in advancing space research. It explores emerging trends and technologies, such as AI-powered spacecraft, swarm robotics, and collaborative AI networks, that hold promise for pushing the boundaries of space exploration. It emphasizes the need for continued research and development to harness the full potential of AI in unraveling the mysteries of the universe.

Conclusion:

This chapter provides a captivating exploration of the intersection between AI and space exploration. By showcasing the application of AI in autonomous rovers, data analysis, astronomical research, and addressing ethical considerations, readers gain insights into the transformative power of AI in advancing our understanding of the cosmos. The chapter also offers a glimpse into the exciting future of AI in pushing the boundaries of space research.

Thank you for joining us on this exploration of Artificial Intelligence. We hope this book has provided you with a comprehensive understanding of AI and its implications.

Thank You

Dear readers of "What is AI,"

I want to express my sincere gratitude to each and every one of you for joining me on this educational and exciting voyage. Your enthusiasm and support have been truly inspiring. I hope this book has shed light on the intricacies of AI and empowered you to embrace the future of this remarkable field. Thank you for being a part of this incredible journey!

Warm regards,

-Ajinkya Khamitkar

Publisher: DeepLata Technologies

To get digital copy in pdf Visit:

www.deeplatatechnologies.com

www.theviral247.com

www.plaatashop.com

or contact on WhatsApp: 9309338947

Contribute to the Author:

If you like the content and information you can contribute and help the author

Scan this QR code to
contribute to the Author